Aimee's **A** Book

WRITTEN BY **J. L. MAZZEO**
ILLUSTRATED BY **HELEN ROSS REVUTSKY**

dingles&company New Jersey

First Printing

Published By dingles&company
P.O. Box 508
Sea Girt, New Jersey 08750

LIBRARY OF CONGRESS CATALOG CARD NUMBER
2005931942

ISBN
1-59646-416-X

Printed in the United States of America

My Letter Library series is based on the original concept of Judy Mazzeo Zocchi.

ART DIRECTION
Barbie Lambert & Rizco Design
DESIGN
Rizco Design
EDITED BY
Andrea Curley
PROJECT MANAGER
Lisa Aldorasi
EDUCATIONAL CONSULTANT
Maura Ruane McKenna
PRE-PRESS BY
Pixel Graphics

EXPLORE THE LETTERS OF THE ALPHABET WITH MY LETTER LIBRARY*

Aimee's **A** Book
Bebe's **B** Book
Cassie's **C** Book
Delia's **D** Book
Emma's **E** Book
Faye's **F** Book
George's **G** Book
Henry's **H** Book
Izzy's **I** Book
Jade's **J** Book
Kelsey's **K** Book
Logan's **L** Book
Mia's **M** Book
Nate's **N** Book
Owen's **O** Book
Peter's **P** Book
Quinn's **Q** Book
Rosie's **R** Book
Sofie's **S** Book
Tad's **T** Book
Uri's **U** Book
Vera's **V** Book
Will's **W** Book
Xavia's **X** Book
Yola's **Y** Book
Zach's **Z** Book

* All titles also available in bilingual English/Spanish versions.

WEBSITE
www.dingles.com
E-MAIL
info@dingles.com

My **Letter** Library

Aa

My Letter Library leads young children through the alphabet one letter at a time. By focusing on an individual letter in each book, the series allows youngsters to identify and absorb the concept of each letter thoroughly before being introduced to the next. In addition, it invites them to look around and discover where objects beginning with the specific letter appear in their own world.

Aa

A a B b C c D d E e F f G g

H h I i J j K k L l M m N n

O o P p Q q R r S s T t U u

V v W w X x Y y Z z

A is for Aimee.

Aimee is an **a**rtistic **a**pe.

At Aimee's afternoon outing

you will find an **a**nt,

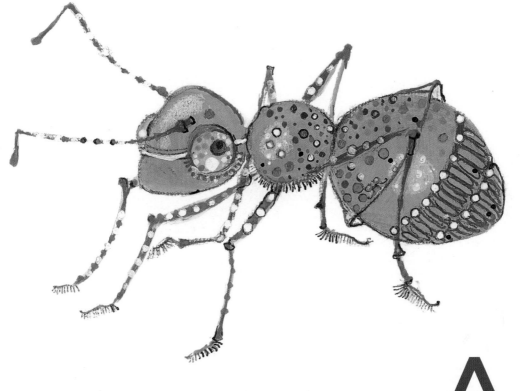

Aa

an **a**corn,

Aa

and **a**rt supplies

for painting.

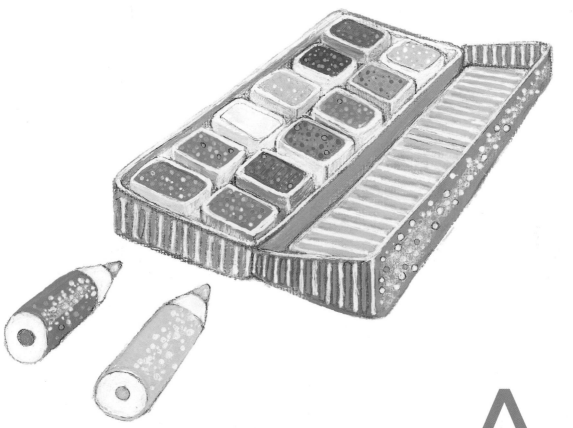

Aa

While having lunch
with Aimee you can
eat **al**monds,

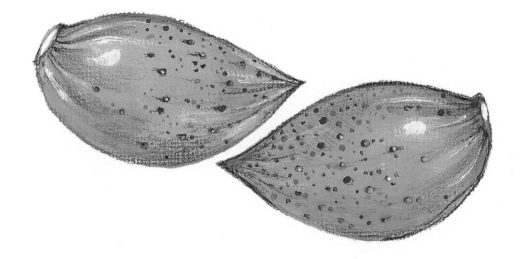

Aa

an appetizing **a**pple,

Aa

or a juicy **a**pricot.

Aa

After eating

at Aimee's outing

you can paint a picture

of an **a**irplane,

Aa

an adorable **a**lligator,

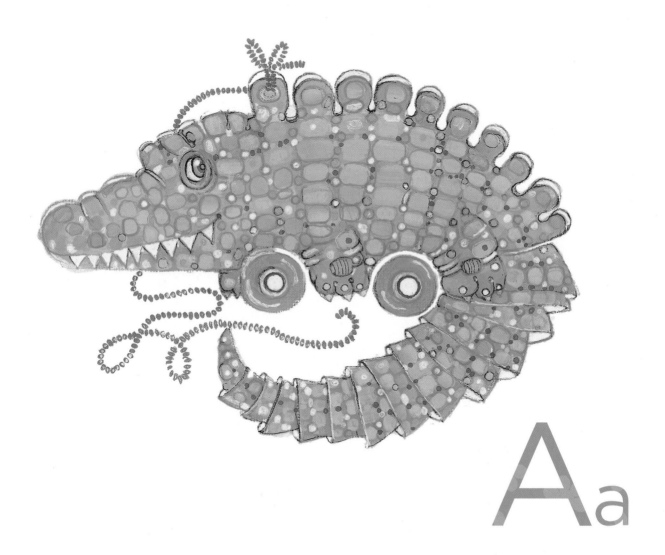

Aa

or an **a**nchor that came
from a tugboat.

Aa

Things that begin with
the letter **A** are all around.

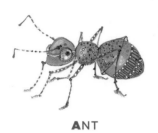

ANT

ACORN

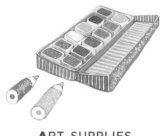

ART SUPPLIES

ALMONDS

APPLE

APRICOT

AIRPLANE

ALLIGATOR

ANCHOR

Where at Aimee's outing
can they be found?

Have an **"A"** Day!

Read "A" stories all day long.
Read books about apes, ants, airplanes, art, apples, and other **A** words. Then have the child pick out all of the words and pictures starting with the letter **A**.

Make an "A" Craft: Apple Prints
Cut any type of apple in half lengthwise.

While you are cutting the apple, discuss different types of apples as well as their tastes and colors.

Place some red, yellow, and green tempera paint on separate paper plates.

Dip an apple half (flat side down) into one of the paint colors.

Then "stamp" the apple half on a piece of construction paper.

Wash the apple before placing it in a different color.

Using the apple like a stamp, make colorful **"A"** apple prints!

Make an "A" Snack: Apple Juice
- Pare an apple.
- Cut the apple into slices.
- Put at least 3/4 cup of sliced apples into a blender.
- Add 1 cup of water and 1 teaspoon of sugar.
- Blend thoroughly and strain if necessary.
- Chill and enjoy!

For additional **"A"** Day ideas and a reading list, go to www.dingles.com.

About **Letters**

Use the My Letter Library series to teach a child to identify letters and recognize the sounds they make by hearing them used and repeated in each story.

Ask:
- What letter is this book about?
- Can you name all of the **A** pictures on each page?
- Which **A** picture is your favorite? Why?
- Can you find all of the words in this book that begin with the letter **A**?

ENVIRONMENT
Discuss objects that begin with the letter **A** in the child's immediate surroundings and environment.

Use these questions to further the conversation:
- Have you tasted any of the fruits mentioned in this book?
- Do you watch airplanes fly through the sky?
- Did you ever see acorns or apples hanging on trees?
- Do you have any art supplies?

OBSERVATIONS
The My Letter Library series can be used to enhance the child's imagination. Encourage the child to look around and tell you what he or she sees.

Ask:
- Do you paint pictures like Aimee does?
- If so, what kind of objects do you like to paint?
- Did you ever want to start an ant farm?
- Where do alligators live?
- Where do apes live?

TRY SOMETHING NEW...
Do you know anyone who is in the hospital? Why not paint that person a picture to brighten up his or her room!

J. L. MAZZEO grew up in Middletown, New Jersey, as part of a close-knit Italian American family. She currently resides in Monmouth County, New Jersey, and still remains close to family members in heart and home.

HELEN ROSS REVUTSKY was born in St. Petersburg, Russia, where she received a degree in stage artistry/design. She worked as the directing artist in Kiev's famous Governmental Puppet Theatre. Her first book, *I Can Read the Alphabet,* was published in Moscow in 1998. Helen now lives in London, where she has illustrated several children's books.